BANDSLAM

Adapted by Aaron Rosenberg

Based on the screenplay by Josh A. Cagan and Todd Graff

LEVEL 2

SCHOLASTIC

Adapted by: Vicky Shipton
Publisher: Jacquie Bloese
Editor: Fiona Davis
Designer: Christine Cox
Picture research: Pupak Navabpour

Photo credits:
Page 5: Aerial Archives/Alamy.
Pages 50 & 51: B Green, AP/Press Association Images; Pictorial Press/Alamy.
Pages 52 & 53: K McKay/Rex; A Warzawa/Corbis; J Goff/ Press Association Images; J Shearer/Getty Images

www.nick.co.uk/bandslam

Copyright © 2010 Summit Entertainment, LLC and Walden Media, LLC. All Rights Reserved. Artwork © 2010 Summit Entertainment, LLC and Walden Media, LLC. All Rights Reserved.

Published by Scholastic Ltd. 2010

No part of this publication may be reproduced in whole or in part, or stored in a retrieval system, or transmitted in any form or by any means, electronic, mechanical, photocopying, recording or otherwise, without written permission of the publisher. For information regarding permission write to:

Mary Glasgow Magazines (Scholastic Ltd.)
Euston House
24 Eversholt Street
London NW1 IDB

Printed in Singapore
This edition printed in 2011.

CONTENTS

	PAGE
Bandslam	**4–47**
People and places	4
Prologue: Monday morning	6
Chapter 1: A new school	8
Chapter 2: The band	13
Chapter 3: I Can't Go On, I'll Go On	20
Chapter 4: Will's favourite place	24
Chapter 5: Sa5m	29
Chapter 6: 'Phil's Song'	33
Chapter 7: Bandslam!	40
Epilogue: 'Dear Will Burton …'	46
Fact Files	**48–53**
The stars of *Bandslam*	48
The music of *Bandslam*	50
Becoming a star	52
Self-Study Activities	**54–56**
New Words	**inside back cover**

PEOPLE AND PLACES

BANDSLAM

Will Burton doesn't have any friends. Instead he has music! He loves all kinds of music and knows almost everything about it. Will lives with his mum, Karen.

Karen Burton knows Will is unhappy at school. She gets a new job so they can move to New Jersey for a new life.

Sam is the first person that Will meets at his new school. She loves reading. She writes her name as *Sa5m*. But the 5 is silent!

Charlotte is beautiful and very cool. So why does she want to hang out with Will?

Ben Wheatly and Glory Dogs are a popular rock band from Will's new school. They want to win Bandslam.

British singer **David Bowie** is one of the most famous musicians in the world. He is Will's hero. Will often writes emails to him.

Bandslam is a big competition for High School rock bands in the east of the USA.

Places

New Jersey Karen and Will move to New Jersey on the east coast of the USA. New Jersey is close to New York.

CBGB This little music club in New York became the centre of American punk rock in the 1970s.

PROLOGUE
Monday morning

 Dear David Bowie
It's Monday morning. So what's new? Here in Cincinnati*, it always feels like Monday morning.

'You're going to be late,' said Will's mum, Karen. 'Are you writing another email to David Bowie?'

Will Burton was in his bedroom. He was sitting at his computer. There were pictures of bands everywhere: new British bands, cool old bands from the 1960s and punk bands. Bowie was Will's hero.

'Don't you care that he never replies?' asked Karen.
'No!' answered Will. 'He doesn't need to reply.'

* * *

Music meant everything to Will. At school some kids liked rap music – but only the most popular rap music. Some rich kids dressed like guys from Jamaican bands, but they didn't know much about the music. No one knew as much about music as Will.

At the end of another long day, Will walked alone to the school bus. Suddenly an older boy ran into him and pushed him over. It was no accident. The kid looked down at Will.

'Sorry!' he laughed. 'I didn't see you there, Dewey!'

* Cincinnati is a large city in Ohio in the USA.

Nobody called Will by his real name. Everybody called him 'Dewey'. Will hated this name more than anything in the world.

Will sat at the side of the road. A hand with a bag of water appeared out of the bus window. The water fell on Will's head. He didn't move. This was just another Monday.

Karen was waiting at the bus stop. 'What can I say to make things better?' she asked.

'Say you've left your job and we're moving out of Cincinnati,' said Will.

Karen smiled. 'I've left my job and we're moving out of Cincinnati!'

'That's not funny, Mum!' Will didn't believe her.

'No, really! I've got a new job in New Jersey!'

Will was interested now. 'Really? That's fantastic!'

New Jersey was far from here. But Will's smile quickly disappeared. 'Life won't be different there, will it?' he said sadly.

'There'll be different people,' said Karen.

'Yes ... but I'll be the same me.'

CHAPTER 1
A new school

 Dear David Bowie
I've started at my new school in New Jersey. There's one good thing about it – nobody knows me here.

It was Will's first day at his new school. As he walked inside with all the other kids, his mobile phone rang. It was his mum.

'What do you think?' Karen asked.

'Don't worry, Mum!' he said. 'It's OK.'

'I told you!' she said happily. 'This school is going to be different!'

Will looked around. He was hundreds of miles from Cincinnati, but the school and the kids looked just the same.

But there *was* something different about this school. During lunch, a student stood up in front of everybody. 'Welcome back to school!' he shouted. 'What's going to happen 3600 hours from now?'

'Bandslam!' everyone shouted.

'And who's going to win?' asked the student with the microphone.

Most of the students were on their feet now. Even the teachers were shouting.

'Ben Wheatly and Glory Dogs!'

Will watched, mouth open, as a rock band came on to a stage at the back of the room and started playing. Ben Wheatly was some sort of school hero. He was a tall, good-looking kid with an easy smile. He looked like the sort of popular kid that Will could never be.

Only one other student – a girl with dark hair – was not looking at the stage. She was reading a book as she ate lunch alone. Will went over to her.

'What's Bandslam?' he asked.

'It's a competition for school rock bands,' she said in a bored voice. 'The winner gets a record deal. Last year Glory Dogs came second.'

'It's really important to people around here, right?'

'More important than football,' she said without looking up from her book. 'You're new here, aren't you? Let me see what classes you're in.'

Will showed her.

'We have Social Studies together,' she said. 'What's your name?'

'Will Burton,' he told her. 'What's yours?'

The girl took out a pen and wrote: *Sa5m*. 'The 5 is silent,' she told him. Then she picked up her book and left.

* * *

'We're going to do an exciting project,' the Social Studies teacher, Ms Wittenberg, told the class. Then she said the words that Will really didn't want to hear. 'I want everyone to choose a partner to work with!'

Ms Wittenberg smiled. 'Find out about your partner and then tell us about them. You can use photos or film. You can draw or sing or write ... but show us who your partner really is!'

All around Will, kids were finding partners. He looked across at Sam. She didn't look very happy. But she had no choice.

After school, they met at the shopping centre to talk about the project. Sam was reading again.

'Do you want to start?' asked Will.

Sam didn't look up. 'What's your favourite colour?' she asked. She didn't sound very interested.

'We have to go deeper than that, I think!' said Will. 'Let's see ... what's your favourite place in the world?'

'Can I think about that?' said Sam.

'OK,' said Will. 'What place do you really *not* like?'

Two noisy teenagers walked past. One of them dropped an empty cup on the floor.

'Here,' she said.

'This isn't going to be easy,' Will thought to himself.

***

The next day, Will got a real surprise. He was walking out of school when somebody shouted, 'Hey, you! Do you like children?'

Will looked up and couldn't believe his eyes. Why was this beautiful, blonde girl talking to him? Girls like her never talked to boys like him!

'What?' he said.

'It's an easy question,' answered the girl. 'Are you good with kids? Come with me!'

Will didn't understand, but he followed her to a noisy classroom full of young children.

'We run an after-school club for young kids,' the girl told him. 'I need some help!'

Will could see that. Some of the children were running. Others were fighting. Lots were shouting.

'Name?' the blonde girl asked.

'Will Burton.'

'Charlotte Barnes. Give me that.' She took Will's MP3 player out of his pocket and turned to the children. 'This is Will,' she said. 'Do you want to hear his music?'

'Yes!' they shouted.

She put the music on – it was a love song from the 1960s. Charlotte looked at Will. She was surprised – this wasn't the kind of music that most teenagers liked!

'They won't want to listen to that!' cried Will. He felt stupid.

'Look!' said Charlotte.

Will looked. The children weren't fighting or running now. They were all quietly working at their desks.

Charlotte smiled. 'They love it.' She turned to him. 'You're a bit strange, aren't you, Will Burton?'

When Will got home that night, he told his mum about Charlotte.

'So what's she like?' she asked.

'She's not just the coolest person who's ever spoken to me,' said Will. 'She's possibly the coolest person in the world!'

'Is she pretty?' asked Karen.

'Mum, we are not going to sit here and talk about girls!' Will picked up his computer and left the room. But he couldn't get Charlotte out of his head.

CHAPTER 2
The band

 Dear David Bowie
Today was really strange … .

Will was walking home from school and listening to his MP3 player. A car slowed down next to him. Charlotte was driving. 'Do you want to see the coolest place ever?' she called through the open window.

A short drive later, Charlotte stopped the car. She got out and sat on the front of it. Will sat next to her, but he didn't feel very comfortable. They could see the tall buildings of the city across the river.

'This is the Overlook. My dad, Phil, brought me here a lot,' Charlotte said.

'*Brought*?' said Will. 'Is he dead?'

'No!' Charlotte cried, suddenly upset. 'Don't say that!'

Will was surprised. 'Sorry!'

Charlotte was quiet for a moment. 'No, *I'm* sorry. My dad got ill last summer. I don't want any more bad luck.'

She jumped off the front of the car and started looking for a CD.

'Can I ask something?' said Will. 'Why are you hanging out with me?'

'Why are you asking why?' said Charlotte.

Will didn't reply. Charlotte pushed the CD into the car's player. 'OK, we need to teach you about music, so we'll start with the best: The Velvet Underground*.'

Will reached for the CD box. 'If we're starting with The Velvet Underground, I prefer the band's songs from *1969*.'

Charlotte was surprised. 'Who *are* you?'

'Will!' he said. He didn't know what else to say.

'Do you know a lot about music?' Charlotte asked.

'Yes.'

'Why didn't you tell me this before?' she asked.

'We didn't really have a "before".' Will gave the CD box back. 'My dad's a musician.'

'No way! Have I heard of him?'

'In the music business, the word for people like him is a 'sideman'. For example, if The Who** need another player on stage ... .'

Charlotte couldn't believe this. 'Does your dad play with The Who?'

'It sounds cool,' said Will, 'but it just means that he's never around. That's why my mum left him.'

'I'm starting a new band,' said Charlotte suddenly. 'We practise at my house on Saturdays – come and listen. You know so much about music. You can help us!'

* The Velvet Underground are a band from the late 1960s. See page 50.

** The Who are a famous British band. They started in the early 1960s.

'I'm not good in groups,' said Will.

Charlotte looked at him. 'Always do what you find most scary.'

It was Saturday. Charlotte's band was practising in her garage. Will looked through the window. The band was just three people – Charlotte and two kids from her year. The guys on guitar, Omar and Bug, jumped around a lot and played really loudly. The band just used a computer for drums. Charlotte sang and played guitar. She stood at the microphone, eyes closed, and sang a song from the 1970s, 'I Want You to Want Me.*'

Charlotte sang well, but something about the band wasn't right. They didn't seem to work together.

Bug saw Will. 'Who's this?' he said angrily.

Charlotte just smiled. 'This is Will! He knows everything

* American rock band Cheap Trick brought out this song in 1977.

about music.' She turned to him. 'So what did you think?'

Will felt uncomfortable. What could he say?

Bug spoke first. 'It was cool, right? The way my bass followed his guitar?' He and Omar waved their guitars around excitedly.

'Look,' said Will. He didn't want to say this, but he couldn't lie – not about music. 'I see what you're trying to do, but it's not really working.'

'What else?' Charlotte asked Will.

'You guys need a real drummer,' he said.

The others were silent. Will tried to think of something else to say.

'What's the band's name?' he asked.

'We're Glory Dogs,' Charlotte said.

Will didn't understand. 'Isn't that the name of the other band?'

'No!' said Bug angrily. 'They're Ben Wheatly and Glory Dogs, like Bruce Springsteen and the E Street Band*. Then Ben can push people out and it's still his band.'

Now Will understood. 'Did you guys play with Ben Wheatly before?' he asked.

'Yes,' said Charlotte. She started to leave. 'Band practice is every Saturday,' she shouted to Will. 'Come back next week and don't be late!'

* * *

After the next Social Studies class, Sam came up to Will.

'We need to meet up for our project,' she said. She didn't look at Will.

'What about your house?' Will said. 'Can you have friends there?'

---

* Bruce Springsteen is the most famous singer from New Jersey.

'Friends,' said Sam carefully. 'I don't have those.'
'I know what you mean,' said Will.
Sam looked at him. 'Maybe we could *not* have friends together.'

But Will had to tell someone about Charlotte. 'Maybe I have one friend,' he said. 'Do you know Charlotte Barnes?'
'Yes, I know her,' said Sam slowly.
'She seems nice. Are you friends with her?'
'No way!' said Sam. 'Cheerleaders don't change.'
'Is she a cheerleader?' Will was surprised.
'She was top cheerleader last year,' said Sam.
'Wow!' Will said. 'She's never talked about it.'

Will didn't understand why, but Charlotte was still hanging out with him. She wanted him to come and see the guys from the band again. This time they met at the café where Charlotte worked.

In the car outside, Will asked her, 'Were you the school's top cheerleader?'

'That was last year,' said Charlotte. She quickly talked about something else. 'Hey! You haven't said anything about my singing. Am I *so* bad?'

'No! You're fantastic!' cried Will.

Charlotte looked at him. 'Are you in love with me?'

'No, I'm not!' said Will.

But it was clear that Charlotte didn't believe him.

Inside the café, Will sat with Bug and Omar. Charlotte was taking water to the tables. Suddenly she stopped. Will looked up and saw Ben Wheatly.

'Hey, Charlotte!' Ben said. Charlotte didn't answer. He joined Bug and Omar. 'How are you?' he asked.

Charlotte walked over. 'Don't talk to him,' she said angrily.

Ben was still smiling. 'Why? What did I do?'

'Have you hit your head and forgotten everything?' asked Charlotte. 'You didn't want them in the band anymore!'

'I found some even better players,' Ben explained. He turned to Bug and Omar. 'You understand that, right? You guys are really good, but sometimes good isn't enough. We have to be great.'

Charlotte turned away. 'I have to work.'

Ben jumped up to follow her. 'Why are you being like this? You left the band before any of this happened!'

Charlotte turned to face him. 'Oh, now I understand,' thought Will. Ben was Charlotte's boyfriend before.

'Can we just go somewhere and talk?' Ben asked her. 'Tomorrow, after school?'

'I'm hanging out with Will,' Charlotte told him.

'Who's Will?' Ben was starting to sound angry.

'That's Will,' said Charlotte pointing.

Ben took one look. Clearly he didn't like what he saw. 'You're joking!' he said to Charlotte.

'Will's my friend,' said Charlotte angrily, 'and the manager of my band.'

Ben looked surprised. Omar and Bug looked surprised. But Will was the most surprised of all. *Manager* of the band?

'Yes,' said Charlotte. 'We have a band, and we're going to Bandslam too.'

'I don't believe it!' said Ben. 'You've changed Charlotte. That's what everyone is saying.'

'Everyone's right,' she said coldly.

CHAPTER 3
I Can't Go On, I'll Go On

 Dear David Bowie
Big news! Life in New Jersey is not completely terrible!

Will couldn't believe it. He was manager of Charlotte's band! This was something that he really wanted to do. His first job was to get a real drummer. But there was only one drummer Bug and Omar wanted.

Basher Martin was famous as the best drummer in the school, but he was also very scary. He could become very angry very quickly ... about anything.

When Will went to see him, Basher was working on a car in the school garage. It wasn't going well and Basher was angry. His long hair fell across his face as he hit the car again and again.

Will almost turned and ran. 'Drums!' he said quickly.

Basher looked up. 'What about them?'

Will spoke too fast. 'My name is Will. I'm the manager of this great new band and we need a drummer for Bandslam.'

'I hate Bandslam!' shouted Basher. 'Everyone wants the record deal, and nobody really cares about music!' He hit the car again.

'I care about music!' cried Will. He moved closer to Basher. 'I know you do too.'

Basher didn't look very sure, but at that moment they heard the sound of an old Bowie song. It was Will's mobile phone.

As Will answered, Basher saw the photo of Karen on the phone. 'Who's that?' he said. 'I like older girls. They understand me.'

'That's my ... .' Will stopped himself. 'That's my older sister,' he lied. 'She hangs out with the band all the time.'

Basher smiled.

* * *

With Basher on the drums, the band sounded much better. But Will wanted more. 'We still need a bigger sound,' he told the band. 'We need more players.'

The next week was busier than ever. 'The band needs some brass,' Will thought to himself. He watched the school band at the football game and chose the best players. Next he went to the music practice rooms. There weren't any rock players there, but Will found some good musicians – a piano player and even a cello player.

At last the band, with all its new players, met to practise. They sat quietly and waited. Everybody seemed to be thinking, 'Why am I here?'

'All of you can give something to this band,' Will told them. 'Let's start. Basher, can you play something simple?'

Basher didn't move.

'Please?'

Basher didn't like to play quietly, but he finally sat at his drums and started to play.

Will turned to Bug. 'OK, now listen to the drums and just play your bass against it.'

With drums and bass playing, Will asked everybody to join in. 'Just listen. Play something that fits the music.'

As each new player joined in, they worked with the others. They were starting to sound like a real band.

'Will Burton, you are fantastic!' said Charlotte.

Will was listening to ska* music on his MP3 player. He gave the player to Sam to listen. She smiled.

'That's cool,' she said. 'But Will, we have to do our project.'

'We'll meet up soon,' said Will. 'I promise. But I really have to work on Charlotte's band right now.'

'You don't have to,' said Sam. 'You want to.'

'You haven't heard them! Believe me – I have to.'

Sam looked away. 'You want to,' she said softly.

After practice, the band met as usual at the café.

'We have to talk about the band's name,' said Will. 'There can't be two Glory Dogs.'

'*We* are Glory Dogs, not them!' said Bug and Omar. They felt strongly about this.

* See Fact File on page 50.

'It's a bad name anyway!' said Will.
'OK,' said Bug crossly, 'what do *you* want to call us?'
Will looked from face to face. 'I Can't Go On, I'll Go On.*'

'What?' cried Bug. 'That's stupid! It's not even a name! We're still Glory Dogs!'

Charlotte joined the table. 'Forget it! Will knows more about music than any of us! His dad plays with famous bands. We were a joke before Will came!' She picked up a glass of water. 'Let's drink to I Can't Go On, I'll Go On.'

* 'I can't go on, I'll go on' is the last line from *The Unnamable* by Samuel Beckett (1953).

CHAPTER 4
Will's favourite place

 Dear David Bowie
You're not going to believe what just happened to me … .

'We haven't hung out since you became Mr Rock Star,' Sam told Will at school. 'We still haven't done that project, and you haven't shown me your favourite place.'

'That's because I haven't been there yet,' said Will.

At the weekend Will and Sam took the train into New York. The city wasn't far from their part of New Jersey. It was like a different world. They went to a great music shop and a great bookshop. They took photos of each other and laughed. They had lunch in Central Park, the most famous park in the world. In the afternoon they went to Will's favourite place.

'This is CBGB,' he said. They were standing outside an empty building. 'This was the most important music club in the last forty years ... and now it's closed.'

The club didn't look good. There were locks on the doors and windows.

Sam didn't really understand why this place was so special for Will. 'Maybe it's better that way,' she said.

Suddenly Sam saw something. There was no lock on one of the doors. She pulled the door open.

'What are you doing?' Will looked around. Was anyone watching them?

Sam just smiled. 'Come on!'

Moments later, they were inside. It was dark and dirty,

but the bar and tables and chairs were still there. There were pictures of bands all over the walls.

'Look at it!' Will said softly.

'It's just an empty building,' said Sam, 'and it smells!'

'Are you joking?' cried Will. 'Punk music was born here!' He ran his hand across the pictures on the walls and read the bands' names. 'The Ramones … Patti Smith … ! Without this place, there could be no Sex Pistols or The Clash*! Without them, there could be no U2, and without U2 there could be no bands like The Killers! It's a long line and it all started here!'

Sam watched Will as he talked excitedly about music. She was really starting to like him. He stopped and looked at her. 'So this is my favourite place. What's yours?'

'Right now?' Sam smiled as her eyes met Will's. 'It's here.'

* The Ramones and Patti Smith were famous US punk musicians (see page 51). The Sex Pistols and The Clash were the two most famous British punk bands in the 1970s.

After the next band practice, Charlotte drove Will home. She stopped outside his house.

'What's happening with you and Sam?' she asked smiling.

'She's my friend,' said Will.

'You like her more than a friend! Have you kissed yet?'

'No!'

Charlotte's smile disappeared. 'Have you ever kissed a girl?'

Will did not want to have this conversation. 'I don't want her to laugh at me,' he said at last.

Charlotte thought for a moment. 'OK,' she said. 'I want you to understand – this is just a lesson. It doesn't mean anything. Now just do what I say. I'm Sam, OK? Start by moving a piece of hair from her face.'

Will stayed very still.

'Go on!' said Charlotte.

Carefully Will moved a piece of Charlotte's blonde hair.

Charlotte continued, 'Now keep your hand there, behind her head. Move your face towards hers ... .'

Will moved towards Charlotte.

'Slowly!' Charlotte said. 'And then ... .' Charlotte came closer and they kissed. Charlotte pulled away first. 'There! That was easy!'

But Will didn't know what to think. Karen didn't know what to think either. She was watching everything from the window.

* * *

After school the next day, Will and Sam sat together at the Overlook. Sam was reading a book again. Next to her, Will was trying to remember Charlotte's instructions about kissing. What was first? Oh yes, the hair ... .

He moved a hand slowly towards Sam, then stopped. She was wearing a hat! He quickly pushed off her hat.

'What are you doing?' asked Sam.

Will tried to think. What now? He put a hand on her head, then moved it around. Was this right? It didn't seem right! Sam hid behind her book again.

It was now or never! Will tried to pull the book out of Sam's hands. Sam held on to it. This was all going wrong! Will tried again and this time threw the book down. He looked into Sam's eyes. Slowly he moved towards her. She didn't move away. Suddenly everything felt right. Their eyes closed and they kissed – a long, soft kiss.

'Do you like scary films?' Sam said suddenly.

Will couldn't speak.

'My favourite is on at the cinema on Saturday,' continued Sam. 'Do you want to go?'

'Sure,' said Will.

The next day, Charlotte had some exciting news. She had tickets to see The Burning Hotels.

'They're one of the favourite bands to win Bandslam!' she said. 'We can see how good they are.'

Will looked at the tickets in her hand. 'That's fantastic!' he said. The concert was on Saturday night.

It was Saturday night. The band was already on stage, and the theatre was full of people. Will pushed his way to the front of the crowd. The music was so loud he could feel it. He began to dance and lost himself in the music.

Sam sat outside the cinema alone. She looked at her watch. Will was late. Where could he be? People were already going into the cinema. Sam just sat and waited. Will still wasn't there. Finally Sam stood up and walked home alone.

CHAPTER 5
Sa5m

Dear David Bowie
I can't believe I let this happen.

At school on Monday morning, Sam wasn't sad anymore. She was angry.

Will tried to explain. 'I'm really sorry! I was stupid! But I had to go and see The Burning Hotels. They'll be at Bandslam!'

Sam didn't want to listen. 'Tell me one thing,' she said. 'Were you with *her*?'

Will knew who she meant. 'Yes.'

This answer clearly hurt Sam. 'Are you in love with Charlotte?'

'What? No!'

Sam pushed past Will. She stopped at the door and said, 'Just remember – she's trouble. Girls like her always are.'

* * *

After school, Will went to Sam's house. She wasn't there yet. Will told her mother about their school project.

'It's about Sam,' said Will. 'I have to show the class who Sam really is.'

Sam's mum thought for a moment. Then she took Will into the living room and put a DVD on. Sam appeared on the TV. She was sitting alone on stage with a guitar. She started singing 'Everything I Own', a slow song by the band Bread*. Sam never looked up as she sang, but her voice was clear and beautiful.

'It was a competition,' explained Sam's mum. 'She didn't win.'

Suddenly a door opened behind them.

'What are you doing?' cried Sam. She turned the TV off. 'I can't believe that you showed him that, Mum!' She looked angrily at Will. 'Why are you here?'

'I ... I just wanted to say sorry again.'

'Just go!' she told him.

In Social Studies the next day, it was Sam's turn to tell the class about Will. She went to the front of the room.

'My project is Will Burton,' she said flatly. 'I don't need photos. Instead I need this.' She held up a mirror. 'This is what Will is like,' she said. 'He's a mirror for you. He shows you what you want to see. It's nice for a while. You stop feeling alone. Then you find out he's doing that with everyone.'

Sam was in front of Will now. He could hear the hurt in her voice. 'There's only one person that he can't do it for – himself. Because he doesn't have any idea who he is.'

---

* Bread was a popular American rock band in the 1970s.

She put the mirror carefully down on Will's desk and went back to her chair.

The room was quiet. 'OK,' said Ms Wittenberg at last. 'That was ... interesting. Will, you're next!'

Will walked slowly to the front. After Sam's cold words, this almost didn't feel real. He put the DVD in the player and started to play his film. A word appeared: *Sa5m*.

Then: *The 5 is silent*.

The film opened with Will sitting on the grass with Sam. But it wasn't the real Sam, it was a full-size photo of her! Will opened a drink and held it to her mouth. At the bottom the words appeared:

Her favourite drink

Then the film showed the photo of Sam at the shopping centre. The words said:

Not her favourite place

The film was funny and sweet. At the end, Will danced around and around with the photo of Sam and the words read:

I'm so5rry, Sa5m.

As Sam watched, she tried not to smile. The film was proof – Will understood her. Only a true friend could make something like this.

Will was watching Sam carefully. Their eyes met and Will smiled. Now he knew that everything was OK between them.

CHAPTER 6
'Phil's Song'

 Dear David Bowie
Sometimes you think that everything is going OK.
That's when it all goes really wrong.

Will was going to class the next day when Ben Wheatly walked into him. The half-smile on Ben's face showed that it wasn't an accident.

'Sorry ... Dewey.'

Suddenly Will felt ill at the sound of that name. How did Ben know that? It was like a bad dream. Will tried to walk on, but Ben stayed by his side.

'That's what they called you at your last school, right? I read all about you at the school office. Tell me ... do you still talk to your famous dad much?'

'I don't know what you're talking about,' Will said quietly.

But Ben was right in front of him now. 'Oh, I think that you do, Dewey.'

That night Will didn't want to talk to anybody. He just lay in bed. He felt that his new life was finished. Somebody knew about his secret from the past.

Suddenly the bedroom window opened. It was Charlotte. She climbed into his room.

Will sat up. 'What are you doing?'

'You didn't answer my text messages.'

Will fell back onto the bed. 'I'm thinking about changing schools.'

'No way!' Charlotte pulled something out of her bag. 'If

you change schools, you can't see this!' There was a book in her hand. 'I'll only show this to the manager of my band ... and my best friend.'

She sat on the bed and handed the book to him. Inside, there were lots of songs. Will read the name of one – 'Phil's Song'.

'Is this song for your dad?' Will asked.

'Not *for* him, exactly. It's *about* him – things that he's said to me.'

Will knew that this was important to Charlotte. 'Thanks,' he said.

'So no more talk about changing schools!' said Charlotte. She pushed him back onto the bed. She was laughing.

Just then, Will's mum opened the door. 'What's happening?' Karen said angrily.

Will hid his face in the bed.

'Get off his bed!' Karen ordered Charlotte.

'Wait!' Charlotte jumped up. 'Do you think that Will's my boyfriend?'

'I saw you kiss him in the car,' said Karen coldly.

'I was just helping him.'

Karen's eyes didn't move from Charlotte. 'Do you know what I think? I don't think that you're a true friend of Will's.'

Will sat up. 'I am still here!' he said. 'Mum, will you please stop?'

'No, I'm not going to stop,' Karen said. 'I'm your mum. It's my job.'

'No!' cried Will. 'You need to let me have a life!' He turned to Charlotte. 'And you ... I'm not a manager of a band. I can't do it!' He lay back down and closed his eyes. 'Would you both please leave me alone?'

Karen looked at Charlotte. Charlotte didn't know what to do.

'Get out!' said Karen.

After Charlotte left, Will sat up again. 'Somebody called me "Dewey" today,' he told Karen.

'What?' said Karen. 'How did they find out? I hate them all ... except you. I love you.'

'Yes, but that doesn't mean much,' said Will. 'You loved Dad too.'

'I was only nineteen and he was a drummer!' Karen pulled Will closer. 'But you are everything to me. I promise you – things are going to be fine.'

When Will next saw Charlotte, she was playing piano alone at school. Her song book was open and she was singing 'Phil's Song'. The words meant a lot to her, and Will could hear it in her voice.

As the song finished, Will sat down. He no longer thought about his angry words the night before.

'That's it,' he said. 'That's the song for Bandslam.'

The rest of the band felt the same. When all the band were playing – drums, bass, guitar, cello, piano and brass – it sounded great.

As they practised, everybody was thinking the same thing: maybe, just maybe, they could do it. Maybe they could really win Bandslam.

'Maybe things *are* going to be fine,' Will thought.

* * *

But then it all went wrong.

Will arrived at the after-school club to help Charlotte as usual. A teacher was there instead.

'Where are the kids? Where's Charlotte?' Will asked.

The teacher looked up from his work. 'Her father died,' he said. 'Didn't you know?'

'No,' said Will. He felt empty inside.

* * *

The next day, Karen drove Will to Charlotte's house. Charlotte was outside.

'This was a mistake,' he said. 'She didn't answer my messages.'

'Go and talk to her,' Karen said. 'She needs a friend right now.'

Will got out of the car. 'Charlotte?'

She looked round, but said nothing.

'I'm sorry,' continued Will. 'I tried to call you.'

'I know,' said Charlotte flatly. 'Thanks. What do you want, Will?'

'Just ... to say that I'm here for you.'

'OK.' Charlotte's voice was still cold. 'Listen, Will, I want to be alone right now.'

'No problem.'

'And about the band ... .'

'Don't worry,' said Will. 'We can practise without you. "Phil's Song" will be ready when you're back.' He stopped. 'Or maybe you don't want us to use that song now?'

'No, it's fine,' said Charlotte.

'It's a beautiful song,' continued Will. 'We could sing it for your dad ... .'

'Stop!' cried Charlotte. 'Just stop, Will. I'm not in the band anymore.'

'We'll find another song!' Will cried.

'It's not about the song! I've left the band, OK?'

'Why?'

'Why are you asking why?'

'I have to!' cried Will. 'I just have to!' This was the most important thing in the world for him – he couldn't lose it now! 'Please ... .' he said quietly.

'Do you really want to know?' said Charlotte. 'OK. When my dad got ill last summer, I made a promise. I

told myself, "I'll be different – better and nicer. Just *please*, let my dad live." I was never nice to kids who weren't popular like me. My dad always hated that. So I changed – I left Ben, I left my friends, I left Glory Dogs. I left everything that made me different from people like ... .'

'People like me,' Will finished for her. 'So we were just some kind of game for you.'

'It sounds stupid, I know.'

'Only one thing was stupid – me. Someone like you is never friends with someone like me.' Will turned and started walking away.

Charlotte ran after him. She was crying now. 'Don't talk to me about lying!' she shouted. 'Dewey!'

Will stopped but he did not look back.

'Dewey – that comes from DWI, doesn't it? Your dad was DWI*. So that's why he had to leave home,' continued Charlotte. 'I don't know what's worse. I changed my life because I loved my father so much. But you told lies about

---

* DWI = Driving While Intoxicated. This means driving after going to a bar and drinking.

your father because you couldn't tell people the true story.'

Without another word, Will walked back to the car.

The news hit the rest of the band hard. With no Charlotte, they had no singer. And with no singer, how could they play in Bandslam? Their dream was finished.

Will and Sam sat with Bug, Omar and Basher in the park after school.

'So Charlotte was just playing with everybody,' said Sam.

Will was thinking. 'This is stupid!' he said at last. 'I don't care about Charlotte. It was real for me. Wasn't it real for everyone else?' He jumped up. 'I won't let Charlotte do this to us. We're still playing in Bandslam!'

'It won't work,' Basher shouted at him. 'What song are we going to do?'

'"Phil's Song",' said Will. 'We can still play it. Charlotte said that.'

'And who's going to sing it?'

Will didn't answer. Instead he looked at Sam.

CHAPTER 7
Bandslam!

Dear David Bowie
Tonight is the biggest night of my life.

It was here at last – Bandslam! The music was loud and the theatre was full. Everybody wanted to be near the stage. They shouted for their favourite bands. There were all kinds of bands – rock, rap, punk – and all of them played brilliantly that night. But which was the best? A line of people from the music business had to decide that.

Karen was at the front of the theatre. She was selling T-shirts of the band. She was surprised when Charlotte walked up to her.

'How are the guys?' Charlotte asked.

'They're fine,' Karen answered carefully. She wasn't sure what Charlotte wanted.

'I'll just tell them good luck.' Charlotte turned to go, but Karen followed her backstage.

'Hey!' Karen shouted. ' "Dennis Ardmore" – does that name mean anything to you?'

Charlotte didn't understand. 'No. Why?'

'Dennis Ardmore was a kid about the same age as Will. Will's dad was drinking in the middle of the afternoon – he drank every afternoon – but he got in his car anyway. Dennis was on his way home from school. Will's dad hit and killed him.'

'I heard,' said Charlotte. 'I'm sorry.'

'Yes, and did you hear that Will went to see Dennis's parents? He wanted to say sorry. He was only twelve – but that's the kind of boy Will was. Of course, everybody hated Will's dad. Then when he wasn't around any more, they hated his kid. They made the name Dewey from DWI. I had to take Will away from there. It was terrible. Music was Will's only friend until he met you. So I'm asking you, please don't be his friend. Don't hurt him anymore. He'll never be OK if you leave him twice.'

Charlotte was crying now. 'Will is different from everybody that I know,' she told Karen. 'I want to say sorry because I want him back in my life. I like me when I'm with Will. And I will do anything in the world to be that person again. So please ... don't ask me not to.'

Karen closed her eyes. She wanted Will to be safe. But what was the best way to do that? Karen moved to one side. 'OK,' she said.

Will and the rest of the band waited backstage. They were quiet. All the bands seemed so good.

'We're dead,' said Bug.

'I don't know,' said a voice at the door. 'I hear that *you're* the band to watch.'

It was Charlotte. Nobody said a word to her.

'Listen,' she said, 'about the band ... . I was angry and stupid. I didn't know what I was doing.'

Everybody in the band just looked at the floor.

'I missed you guys,' said Charlotte, 'and I'm sorry.'

It was Will who spoke. 'Do you mean that?'

'Yes! I just want you guys to win tonight with "Phil's Song". I'm going to be right at the front and I'm going to shout for you!'

A DJ jumped on stage and took the microphone. 'And now, from New Jersey,' he cried, 'it's Ben Wheatly and Glory Dogs!'

Ben and the band ran out on stage. When the crowd's shouts died down, Ben took the microphone. 'I'd like to sing this for a very special person,' he said. 'She taught me a lot and she wrote this song. Charlotte, this is for you.' And then he started to sing 'Phil's Song'!

Charlotte was standing next to Karen in the crowd. Karen was looking at her angrily.

'I didn't know!' cried Charlotte. 'I promise you. I wrote that song a long time ago. Ben knew it. He probably thinks that he's doing something nice for me!'

Backstage, Will and the band couldn't believe their ears.

'We can't go on and sing the same song!' cried Bug.

'I don't know any other songs,' said Sam.

Everybody was upset, but Will was thinking fast. 'Yes, you do!' he told Sam. '"Everything I Own" – you sang it in a competition before.'

He turned to the others. 'You *all* know it! It's famous and it's easy to play. Everybody outside – now!'

In the little street behind the theatre, everybody in the band was talking at the same time. Each of them was trying to work out his or her part. They had about five minutes!

Will stood at the door. 'We're on next!' he cried. 'Come on!'

'We need a minute,' Sam told him.

'We don't have a minute,' said Will.

Sam's voice was like a knife. 'We ... need ... another ... minute!'

Inside the theatre, the DJ was on stage. 'Our next band is also from New Jersey! It's ... I Can't Go On, I'll Go On!'

The crowd shouted, but the band didn't appear. The shouts stopped, and still the stage was empty. Finally, one kid walked out onto the stage alone. It was Will. He stood at the microphone but he was unable to get the words out. He just looked out at the crowd in the dark.

After a few seconds, someone called out, 'Dewey!' A few kids laughed, and someone else shouted, 'Dewey!' Soon lots of kids were shouting it. 'Dewey! Dewey!'

Karen was standing in the centre of the crowd. She could do nothing to help her son.

More and more kids were shouting together now. 'Dewey! Dewey! Dewey!'

Will turned and started to hurry off. But then he stopped. He couldn't run away – not again. Slowly he walked back to the microphone. His own voice joined the shouts of the crowd: 'Dewey! Dewey!'

Karen watched Will. What was he doing?

'Come on!' Will was shouting louder now. 'Dewey ... Dewey ... Dewey want to rock?'

'Yes!' shouted the crowd with one voice.

'I said ... *Do we* want to rock?'

'Yes!'

Will saw his band. They were waiting at the side of the stage.

'Because I have seen the future!' he cried. 'And their name is I Can't Go On, I'll Go On!'

The band ran out on stage and began their song. They played it as a ska song and everybody in the band was brilliant.

Sam was a different person now. She danced across the stage with the microphone in her hand. She was fantastic. The crowd loved it, and sang along with all the words. Will danced to the music from the side of the stage. He almost couldn't believe it – this was his band!

At the end of the competition, all of the bands stood on stage. This was the big moment.

The DJ was back at the microphone. 'And the winner of this year's Bandslam is ... .'

Ben waited. Will waited. Time seemed to slow down. Who was the winner?

'From Greenwich High School, it's ... The Daze!'

Will couldn't believe it. After all this time and all this hard work, they didn't win! Then he looked around at the faces of the kids in his band. OK, they weren't the winners, but they were still a great band and they were his friends. Sam came up and smiled at him. He looked into her eyes. Maybe losing wasn't so bad.

EPILOGUE
'Dear Will Burton ...'

Two teenagers from the crowd were leaving Bandslam. One of them looked down at the video of I Can't Go On, I'll Go On on his mobile phone.

'Forget The Daze,' he told his friend. 'These guys were *the best*. I'm going to post this on YouTube*.'

Lots of people watched the video on YouTube. Then they emailed friends and told them to watch it too. Kids from the concert told their friends about the band, and those friends told their friends. More and more people wanted to hear I Can't Go On, I'll Go On.

Soon people from other parts of the country – even other parts of the world – were watching the band! After a couple of weeks, one very special person saw the video on YouTube. He went to the band's website and read more. Then he wrote an email to the band's manager.

* YouTube is a website where users can post and watch videos.

Will was reading his emails on the way to school. He looked at the first one and started to smile. He couldn't believe what he was reading.

 Dear Will Burton,
It says on your website that you're the manager of I Can't Go On, I'll Go On – nice name!
I'm looking for new music and I really like your band. Have you got a record deal yet? Maybe we can discuss this?
All the best,
David Bowie

FACT FILE

THE STARS OF

Bandslam is all about music. So it's no surprise that the three stars are all singers and musicians as well as actors! Here they talk about music, playing Rock Band in the dressing room and kissing!

Vanessa Hudgens (Sam)
"I've played the sweet, nice girl for a while."

Q: Tell us about your character, Sam, in *Bandslam*.
A: In *High School Musical*, I played the sweet, nice girl. It was great but it's a lot like me. Sam is very different to me and that was exciting for me as an actor.

Q: You're a musician and have two albums behind you. Did that help you in *Bandslam*?
A: Yes, but I also felt very nervous! I had to learn to play the guitar for the Bandslam scene. I usually do pop music, not rock with a guitar!

Q: Did you enjoy filming in Austin, Texas?
A: I loved Austin because of its music. When you go out, there's music everywhere. It's really different to my home in Los Angeles.

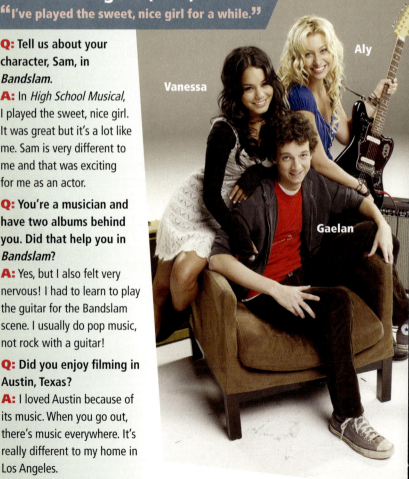

BANDSLAM

Aly Michalka (Charlotte)
"It was like a family."

Q: What was the best thing about working on *Bandslam* for you?
A: There were lots of things, but it was great to hang out with the others. We all spent lots of time together. After filming, we often went out to see a band or have dinner. And we played a lot of Rock Band* in the dressing room! It was like a family.

Q: You have your own band with your sister, AJ. What do you think of the music in *Bandslam*?
A: It's great. There are older hits like 'Everything I Own' but there are new songs too. In the film, I sang 'Amphetamine' by Steve Wynn. It's one of my favourite songs, so that was really cool.

Gaelan Connell (Will)
"I'm a bit like Will in real life!"

Q: Are you like your character, Will, in *Bandslam*?
A: Yes and no! I'm different from Will but we both like the same kind of music. Will's life is all about music. I sing in a band and I play the guitar, but I know a lot more about music now than I did before! Todd, the director, was always giving me new playlists for my ipod and music books to read.

Q: You had to do two different kissing scenes with Vanessa and Aly. Were you nervous?
A: Yes! It was on my first day of filming too! It was really scary for Will and it was scary for me too. I didn't have to act!

* Rock Band is a video game. Players are in a rock band and play hit songs.

Which character in *Bandslam* did you like best and why?

What do these words mean? You can use a dictionary.
character   act / actor   album
nervous   scene   director   playlist

49

FACT FILE

THE MUSIC OF BANDSLAM

From 1950s Jamaican ska to The Burning Hotels, *Bandslam* is full of exciting music. The film takes us from the sounds that influenced music today to the new young bands of tomorrow.

Ska

Will's band, I Can't Go On, I'll Go On, plays 'Everything I Own' at Bandslam. The song was originally by Bread, a rock group. Will's band play it in the style of ska music. Ska music started in Jamaica in the 1950s, with singers like Prince Buster. Ska was also very popular in the late 1970s, with bands like The Specials and Madness. Reggae music came from ska.

Prince Buster

The Velvet Underground

Will and Charlotte both love The Velvet Underground, a New York band from the late 1960s and early 1970s. The band's two main songwriters were Lou Reed and John Cale. The Velvet Underground's songs were often dark and strange. At the time they weren't a popular band, but they had a big influence on later music.

The Velvet Underground

The Ramones

New York Punk Rock

Will's favourite place in the world is CBGB, a little music club in New York. In the 1970s the club became famous for a new kind of music – punk rock. The Ramones, the Patti Smith Group, Television, Talking Heads and Blondie all played there. The club stayed open until 2006. Punk singer Patti Smith was back on stage for the club's last night.

DID YOU KNOW?
Bandslam director, Todd Graff, was once in a band that played at CBGB!

Which bands or music styles would you like to find out more about? Why?

Bandslam bands

Todd Graff filmed *Bandslam* in Austin, Texas. 'There are lots of great bands in Austin,' he says, 'and a lot of them don't have record deals. So they're playing in bars and clubs, and they're on MySpace and YouTube.'

Todd picked five of these bands to be in the Bandslam competition. At the competition, the bands and the actors played in front of a real crowd. Over 1200 people came to watch. One of the young bands in the film was rock band The Burning Hotels.

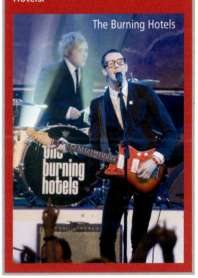
The Burning Hotels

What do these words mean? You can use a dictionary.
influence (n & v)   originally   style
director   actor

FACT FILE

Becoming a star:
Talent shows, downloads or just hard work?

In *Bandslam*, The Daze win a record deal, but Will's band becomes popular from a website video. The Strokes, Radiohead, Lily Allen and Leona Lewis are some big names from the world of music. But how did they get where they are today?

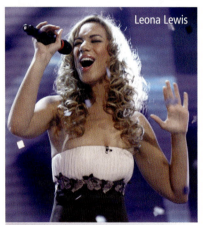
Leona Lewis

Leona Lewis won the popular UK TV talent show *The X Factor* in 2006. Leona wrote her first song at the age of twelve. At seventeen, she wanted to make an album. She took a number of jobs to get enough money. 'I tried to get a record deal by doing things my own way,' she says. 'I worked very hard but I never got one.' Leona finally got her record deal when she won *The X Factor*. Her first album has sold 6.5 million copies around the world.

In 2005, British singer **Lily Allen** put some of her songs on the website MySpace. Her music became more and more popular. Soon she had tens of thousands of followers on the site. Later, she signed a deal with a big music company. Her first album *Alright Still* came out in 2006.

Lily Allen

The Strokes

The New York band **The Strokes** became famous when a small record company gave away a free MP3 download of their song *Last Nite* on a UK music website. Then a few big record companies became interested in the band. Their first album *Is This It* was a hit.

> Who are your favourite bands or singers? How do you usually find out about new music?

Did you know?

In 2007, Radiohead's seventh album, *In Rainbows*, came out as a download only. People could decide how much to pay for the download. Around 33% tried to pay almost nothing, but most people paid a fair price. The album came out on CD months later.

The musicians of British band **Radiohead** met while they were still at school. At first their name was On a Friday because they practised in the school's music room on a Friday. When they left school, the band continued to practise at weekends and in holidays and played concerts around their home town of Oxford.

One of the band members, Colin Greenwood, worked in a record shop. He was lucky to meet someone from the record company EMI in the shop. Shortly after, the band signed a six-album record deal and changed their name to Radiohead.

Radiohead

> What do these words mean? You can use a dictionary.
> talent show   album   record
> company   concert   download

SELF-STUDY ACTIVITIES

PROLOGUE – CHAPTER 2

Before you read

1. Complete the sentences with these words. You can use a dictionary.
   competition   hero   manager   project   silent   stage
   a) You have to be … in the library.
   b) I won a new bike in the … !
   c) We are working on a homework … together.
   d) My mum is the … of the office.
   e) Our school has got a … for shows.
   f) I love dancing! My … is Michael Jackson.

2. Match the words with the sentences. You can use a dictionary.
   bass   cheerleaders   drums   a musician   Social Studies
   a) This person plays music.
   b) This is a school subject.
   c) This guitar makes a deep sound.
   d) You play these by hitting them.
   e) These people shout and dance at sports games.

3. Look at 'People and places' on pages 4–5. Answer the questions.
   a) How does Sam write her name?
   b) What is the name of the band at Will's new school?
   c) Who is the cool girl at Will's new school?
   d) What is the most important thing in Will's life?
   e) What is Bandslam?

After you read

4. Are these sentences true or false? Correct the false sentences.
   a) Singer David Bowie is Will's friend.
   b) Ben Wheatly and his band did not win Bandslam last year.
   c) In Social Studies, Will has to find out more about his parents.
   d) Charlotte asks Will to help with the after-school club.
   e) Will thinks that Charlotte's band needs a bass player.
   f) Bug and Omar played in Ben's band before.

5. What do you think?
   Is Will going to be a good band manager?

CHAPTERS 3-5

Before you read

6 Which do you like best and why?
   brass   cello   drums   guitar   piano

7 Complete the sentences with these words.
   crowd   get ill   kiss   promise   theatre
   a) There's a really good show at the … .
   b) There was a big … of people at the football game.
   c) I'll work harder. I … you.
   d) I feel very cold. I hope that I don't … .
   e) I will always remember our first … .

After you read

8 Put these sentences in order.
   a) Charlotte and Will kiss.
   b) The band gets a new name.
   c) Basher Martin becomes the band's new drummer.
   d) Will shows the class a film about Sam.
   e) Will and Sam go to New York.
   f) Will finds more musicians to join the band.
   g) Will goes to see a band with Charlotte.
   h) Sam and Will kiss.

9 Write the names.
   Basher   Charlotte   Karen   Sam   Will
   a) … hates Bandslam.
   b) Basher sees a photo of … on Will's phone.
   c) Sam wants to see a scary film with … .
   d) … has got tickets to see The Burning Hotels.
   e) … tells the class that Will is like a mirror.
   f) …'s favourite place is CBGB.

10 What do you think?
   Is Will in love with Sam or Charlotte?

SELF-STUDY ACTIVITIES

CHAPTER 6 – EPILOGUE

Before you read

11 What do you think?
   a) Is Will going to stay friends with Sam?
   b) Is Will going to stay friends with Charlotte?
   c) Who will win Bandslam?

After you read

12 Choose the correct words to complete these sentences.
   a) Ben Wheatly finds out the secret about Will's **father** / **mother**.
   b) Charlotte wrote a song about her **mum** / **dad**.
   c) Charlotte leaves the band after her father **dies** / **leaves**.
   d) Will's band **play** / **don't play** 'Phil's Song' in Bandslam.
   e) Sam becomes the band's new **piano player** / **singer**.

13 Who is speaking? Who are they speaking to?
   a) 'Do you still talk to your famous dad much?'
   b) 'I'm thinking about changing schools.'
   c) 'I saw you kiss him in the car.'
   d) 'I changed my life because I loved my father so much.'
   e) 'I'm going to be right at the front and I'm going to shout for you!'
   f) 'Do we want to rock?'

14 Answer the questions.
   Who …
   a) … wants to be friends with Will again?
   b) … sings 'Phil's Song' in Bandslam?
   c) … wins Bandslam?
   d) … puts the video of I Can't Go On, I'll Go On on the website?
   e) … sends Will an email?

15 What do you think?
   a) Who is your favourite person in the story? Why?
   b) What will happen to the band after the end of the story?
   c) Would you like to be in a band? Why or why not?